Gardening

Discover The Complete Extensive Guide On The Best Gardening Techniques And Benefits #1

Gardening

An Easy Guide To Growing Organic Vegetables Easily Using Vertical Gardening

Disclaimer
- Although the author and publisher have made every effort to ensure that the information in this book was correct at press time, the author and publisher do not assume and hereby disclaim any liability to any party for any loss, damage, or disruption caused by errors or omissions, whether such errors or omissions result from negligence, accident, or any other cause.
- This book is not intended as a substitute for the medical advice of physicians. The reader should regularly consult a physician in matters relating to his/her health and particularly with respect to any symptoms that may require diagnosis or medical attention.

Copyright 2014 by LOVE AND LIVE LIFE TO THE EXTREME FULLEST PUBLISHING- All rights reserved.

This document is geared towards providing exact and reliable information in regards to the topic and issue covered. The publication is sold with the idea that the publisher is not required to render accounting, officially permitted, or otherwise, qualified services. If advice is necessary, legal or professional, a practiced individual in the profession should be ordered.

- From a Declaration of Principles which was accepted and approved equally by a Committee of the American Bar Association and a Committee of Publishers and Associations.

In no way is it legal to reproduce, duplicate, or transmit any part of this document in either electronic means or in printed format. Recording of this publication is strictly prohibited and any storage of this document is not allowed unless with written permission from the publisher. All rights reserved.

The information provided herein is stated to be truthful and consistent, in that any liability, in terms of inattention or otherwise, by any usage or abuse of any policies, processes, or directions contained within is the solitary and utter responsibility of the recipient reader. Under no circumstances will any legal responsibility or blame be held against the publisher for any reparation, damages, or monetary loss due to the information herein, either directly or indirectly.

Respective authors own all copyrights not held by the publisher.

The information herein is offered for informational purposes solely, and is universal as so. The presentation of the information is without contract or any type of guarantee assurance.

The trademarks that are used are without any consent, and the publication of the trademark is without permission or backing by the trademark owner. All trademarks and brands within this book are for clarifying purposes only and are the owned by the owners themselves, not affiliated with this document.

Have Any Issues With This Book? Contact Randy at Randycfo@triggerhealthyhabits.com For Any Concerns About Quality, Copyright, Trademark, Or any issues or concerns you may have.

Your FREE Gift
Click Here

As a way of saying thank you,

Get your free natural therapeutic remedies report by clicking below.

What you'll receive

Enjoy the rest of the book!

Click here to get your Natural Therapeutic Remedies Report

The Benefits Of Short Reads,

Our Main Mission Is To Provide You With Quality Content In A Short Period Of Time, We Strive To Make Our Books Short And To The Point. These Days Who Has The Time To Read A Big Long Book? We Do Not Write Fiction Books, We Want To Help As Many People As Possible By Providing Them These Handbooks To Help Better Their Lives. We Hope You Enjoy This Kindle Short Reads E-Book

Table Of Contents

Introduction

Why I Wrote This Book

What You Should Know Before Reading This Book

Chapter 1: Why Organic?

Chapter 2: Easiest Plants To Start With

Chapter 3: What is Vertical Gardening?

Chapter 4: Compost and Fertilizer

Chapter 5: Pest Control

Chapter 6: Seasons and Harvesting

Conclusion

Introduction

Have you ever wanted to try your hand at gardening? If so, then this is the book for you. Sometimes, when you don't have a lot of space, it makes it difficult to find out how you can use your space wisely and the most efficiently. Fortunately, this book is going to help you find out how you can discover all the ways that you can garden in a small amount space. This method is called vertical gardening, and you won't be able to believe just how useful it can be.

Growing your own vegetables and edibles like herbs is one of the most rewarding things you can do. It will save you a lot of money in the long run, and be well worth the time and effort. Not only is gardening useful, but it can be fun and therapeutic as well. If you have ever wanted to say a huge chunk of money on your grocery bill, gardening and growing your own food is the best thing that you will have ever done.

But don't take my word for it! Instead, read this book and find out for yourself exactly how you can utilize the knowledge of vertical gardening and apply it to your own life. You will be amazed. You will save a lot of money, and have a deeper connection with the world around you. Sometimes it takes practice and a little bit of work to get where you want to be in your garden, but the work is always worth it in the payout is incredible. Your garden will pay for itself in both beauty and yield all you have to do is read this book, apply these concepts, and live the life you've always dreamed. Let's get started!

Why I Wrote This Book

I wrote this book because I want people to know that they are empowered no matter how little space they have. Even if they don't feel like they have enough room for a garden, the truth is that you can make the room and yield great results. I know what it's like to live somewhere small, without a lot of space for plants and gardening, so discovering vertical gardening can be a game changer. If you are paying a ton of money every month for fresh fruit and vegetables, when you take the vertical gardening and your space to provide yourself with a plethora of fresh food for free, barring a little bit of work on your part, this is a great solution.

I wrote this book because many people don't know how much power they have to provide healthy, delicious foods for themselves easily and cheaply, and even organically for no cost beyond what time it might take plant the seeds and nurture your vegetables until harvest. I would love for everybody to know that they can produce their own food, and even if they don't have a big yard, or even a yard at all, they can still find a way to make gardening work for them. It's a great opportunity to learn more about nature and stay motivated to connect to your environment. Everybody wants sheep and easy food, and having your own garden makes this very possible.

When it comes to being healthy and active, gardening helps in so many ways. First of all, it gets you out of the house and into the fresh air. You have a lot of plants you will find yourself surrounded by high quality and delicious oxygen freshly emitted from your plants. Another plus time to gardening is that it will help you stay active without being too demanding on the body. Of course it can be a little bit extreme if you have to build your own beds and things like that, but sometimes that is just part of the fun. And to top it all off, you will learn more than you ever thought you would have on growing your own foods, and thousands of dollars as the years progress. So get out there and enjoy the sun while you try out gardening today!

What You Need To Know Before Reading This Book

Before you read this book, you should know that although gardening can be easy, it also takes a lot of dedication. In order for your garden to grow well, going to have to know which things will be compatible so that they don't have to fight for nutrients or sunlight. Sometimes there is some intensive research that can go into having the most successful garden possible, depending on the types of food that you want to grow.

You are also going to need to be careful when it comes to fertilizing your little crops. Each plant requires a specific amount of nutrients, and if you are over fertilizing or under fertilizing them, they are never going to be able to thrive. If you have a clump of plants that need the same type of fertilizer, sometimes it can help the plant then near each other so they you don't accidentally give them the wrong fertilizer and ruin the plant. This can be very sad, so do your best to avoid it when possible.

Another thing is that you will need to be careful with sharp tools like garden spades and shears if you are going to use them. Never use too much force without making sure that none of your body parts are safely out of the way. That being said, it can also be important to take good care of your needs and do exercises that will strengthen them so that intensive gardening doesn't harm your body if you plan to be crouched down in the dirt for a long time. Vertical gardening doesn't have the same downside, but it's a good to keep in mind nonetheless. Overall just remember to have fun and stay positive. Gardening is a wonderful practice and will bring you hours of joy.

Chapter 1: Why Organic?

Has become more popular than ever because of the rise of genetically modified foods and dangerous chemicals leaching into our water supply and the food we eat. These chemicals get on our food when they are used as pesticides in conventional farming. They are very dangerous and can cause cancer and other health problems, especially once the toxins into our bloodstream and start affecting us whether we know they are there or not.

To avoid this mess, we should look toward organic gardening. Organic foods are very expensive to buy, for many reasons, but what this shows is that if you were to grow your own organic food, you would save a lot of money in the long run on groceries that are guaranteed to be healthy and safe for your family. If you don't put chemicals and pesticides into your body, you will have fewer health problems down the line and be very glad that you are not suffering because of the food you ate once you reach a ripe old age.

Organic gardening is not only fine but it is rewarding and economical. It has become advised to eat organic foods whenever possible so that we can avoid these health problems. It is dangerous and unhealthy, especially eating certain foods like blueberries and leafy greens if they have been treated with chemical pesticides rather than organic methods. Because of the high yield of mega-farms, they use even more pesticides. Not only does it get into the plants, but it leaches into the soil and the water. That's dangerous for the entire planet, and their output should be reduced.

Even just one organic garden will decrease the demand in the mega farm industry, and if everybody begins eating organic, they will have no choice but to stop monopolizing them like a very dangerous ways. Once organic food becomes affordable and more accessible than the food from mega-farms, we will see the world start to change for the better. If you want to be a part of that, then this is why you should read this book.

Chapter 2: Easiest Plants to Start With

If you are new to gardening, you will benefit from a list of plants that are easy for beginners to grow successfully in their gardens. These plants are undemanding, useful, and delicious. Many of them actually have herbal medicinal uses and can provide the body's vitamins and nutrients that can reinforce the immune system and keep us healthy.

Herbs like basil, sage, thyme, cilantro, mint, parsley and more, are not only delicious and added to the other foods, but also help detoxify the body and prevent disease. Tomatoes are pretty easy, but they require a lot of water. Tomatoes are always useful and easily grown, and are well matched with the herbs. Potatoes can be simply grown in a barrel, and strawberries grow in abundance once planted.

Greens, including kale, spinach, and arugula easy to grow and maintain garden and great for your health. They provide your body with amazing nutrients that help us function. It can take your choice of peppers, as they are also easy to grow. You will find these vegetables to be great places to start in your organic garden.

Chapter 3: What Is Vertical Gardening

Vertical gardening is a clever way to use space that can allow people who don't have large yards to participate in the fun and rewarding activities related to gardening. To create a vertical garden, you can use shell or craft fun paths that Scott got along the wall. Many people with balconies use vertical gardening to make the most of their limited space. If you are interested in creating a vertical garden, here are the steps you'll need to take.

First of all, decide where you want your garden. It should be along the wall, preferably one that gets a lot of direct sunlight. Gardens require a frame where you can plant foods safely inside. The idea behind the frame is that it makes your garden easy to relocate and maintain when necessary, while taking up unused space that ultimately ends up providing you with nourishment. It is probably better not to use it would because wood can mold, warp, and grow soft.

The same needs to be waterproof, and plastic can often provide this feature. Where you end up putting your plan is going to need to be able to retain water without growing mold. There are some fabrics that you can plant into that will hold the water for you. You'll have to make sure it is well irrigated so that the water reaches all your plants. Depending on the system you use for your irrigation, you can also include liquid fertilizer to be dispersed among your plants. Just make sure that the fertilizer grade is consistent with your plant's needs.

Chapter 4: Compost and Fertilizer

Useful in any garden, and can be made by anybody. Compost is made up of organic plant and food matter that is beginning to break down so that nutrients are ministered into the soil. If you are new to gardening, compost will be your best friend. If you're vertical garden contains pots of soil, you will want to make sure that you include compost into them. You can also make a tea out of compost by watering it down and using that water on your plants.

When it comes to keeping implants healthy, you need 3 essential things. Phosphorus, nitrogen, and potassium. Without these three elements, your plants will not be able to thrive. Because every plant has a different need when it comes to fertilizer, make sure to check your specific plant's requirements before adding fertilizer that may burn it out and harm it.

On the fertilizer, nitrogen indicated with an N, potassium is indicated with a K, phosphorous is indicated with me. Make sure the fertilizer matches your plant's needs before applying it and follow the directions carefully. Otherwise, you may be unpleasantly surprised to find leave of your plant burnt because of the harsh chemical makeup of the fertilizer and unable to continue growing. It is well worth the simple examination of the fertilizer bags to avoid this tragedy.

Chapter 5: Pest Control

One of the biggest challenges to organic gardening is pest control. The biggest is consuming organic foods is that they have not been treated with dangerous pesticides. The downside is that pesticides are needed for a reason, and where bugs find fresh, delicious food, they will feast and make themselves comfortable. Fortunately there are remedies that you can use that are natural and effective against pests.

Most of this involves common sense and a little bit of research. Because there are so many different pests that can affect the garden, make sure that you know exactly what you're dealing with before treating a plant. Sometimes, you can plant certain foods near each other to deter common pests. The option of botanical insecticides is much more gentle than chemical pesticides and will take care of large pest problems.

However, pest control is usually the most effective when you get solutions that are specific to the pest you are dealing with. There are many natural remedies, from apple cider vinegar to onion and garlic peels soaked in water and put in the sun for a few days. As mentioned, look into the specifics of both your plants and the pest for the most effective solution.

Chapter 6: Seasons and Harvesting

You know, there are different seasons for different types of food. Some plants thrive better in certain climates than others, meaning they should be planted during specific times of the year. There is no way to list all of the different plants and seasons in one small book, but the guidelines are basically to know your plant inside and out before you deal with it so that you can have the best yield possible.

Harvesting plants can be difficult if you don't know what you're doing, so depending on your plant make sure you read up on exactly what to do with it. Some things are better to cut off than pull, like tomatoes for example. That way nothing gets torn and bruised. Make sure you know exactly when to harvest, and do your best to know the best time they should be harvested for the best taste. For example, squash plants should be harvested young and allowed to mature off the line. This can be true of tomatoes as well if you are willing to wait, but they do taste better fresh off the vine.

If you have chosen to grow peppers, you can harvest them just about any time and they will taste great. However if you want the best taste, allow them to reach maturity. A good rule of to follow, especially when you have foods like kale and broccoli, is to harvest them young and harvest them frequently. This will keep you in good supply and allow the plans to keep growing and provide you with their maximum output for your yield.

Conclusion

Overall, organic gardening is one of the most rewarding pursuits a person can undergo. All the money we spend on processed foods and pesticide lead in fruits and vegetables can be cut away simply by having your own organic garden. If you are interested in changing the world one garden at a time, and sticking it to the big corporations to try and force us to rely on their unhealthy and poisoned foods, one of the best ways that you could possibly do this is to stop relying on them and start looking at what you can do for yourself and your family. There is no reason anybody would have to be without their own garden, no matter how great or small it may be. Any contribution of free organic food is worthwhile, and will save you money in the long term.

Vertical gardening, you will be able to take up some useless space and turn it into something beautiful. Vertical gardens are not only useful and easy, but they are also extremely aesthetically pleasing. You wouldn't believe how much better a wall looks with living plants hanging on it than it might look bare, without anything to boast. Organic gardening just gets better if you add in the possibilities of a vertical garden.

The best way to ensure success gardening as a beginner is to look into every plant that you want to include in the garden, and every past in your area that might affect them. This way, you can arm yourself with non-chemical insecticides and ways to keep these pests away from your vegetables so that you can enjoy them for yourself. Get to know the foods that you want to grow so that you can harvest at the right time and enjoy them at their peak.

You should set up your own compost in, where you can throw all food, specifically vegetable and fruit residue inside of it to create a nutritious cocktail for your plants. Make sure to regularly stir the compost so that it does not catch fire, and then apply it to your plants as needed. Otherwise you may find the soil losing nutrients and your foods will not grow as well. Overall, just remember to have fun and enjoy this connection that you have made with nature. Knowing exactly where your food comes from is comforting and satisfying, and is a feeling that you will never want to get rid of once you have it. Go out there and have fun, I know you can do it!

Landscaping

Discover 8 Amazing Tips To Make Your Garden Decorative

Disclaimer
- Although the author and publisher have made every effort to ensure that the information in this book was correct at press time, the author and publisher do not assume and hereby disclaim any liability to any party for any loss, damage, or disruption caused by errors or omissions, whether such errors or omissions result from negligence, accident, or any other cause.
- This book is not intended as a substitute for the medical advice of physicians. The reader should regularly consult a physician in matters relating to his/her health and particularly with respect to any symptoms that may require diagnosis or medical attention.

Copyright 2014 by LOVE AND LIVE LIFE TO THE EXTREME FULLEST PUBLISHING- All rights reserved.

This document is geared towards providing exact and reliable information in regards to the topic and issue covered. The publication is sold with the idea that the publisher is not required to render accounting, officially permitted, or otherwise, qualified services. If advice is necessary, legal or professional, a practiced individual in the profession should be ordered.

- From a Declaration of Principles which was accepted and approved equally by a Committee of the American Bar Association and a Committee of Publishers and Associations.

In no way is it legal to reproduce, duplicate, or transmit any part of this document in either electronic means or in printed format. Recording of this publication is strictly prohibited and any storage of this document is not allowed unless with written permission from the publisher. All rights reserved.

The information provided herein is stated to be truthful and consistent, in that any liability, in terms of inattention or otherwise, by any usage or abuse of any policies, processes, or directions contained within is the solitary and utter responsibility of the recipient reader. Under no circumstances will any legal responsibility or blame be held against the publisher for any reparation, damages, or monetary loss due to the information herein, either directly or indirectly.

Respective authors own all copyrights not held by the publisher.

The information herein is offered for informational purposes solely, and is universal as so. The presentation of the information is without contract or any type of guarantee assurance.

The trademarks that are used are without any consent, and the publication of the trademark is without permission or backing by the trademark owner. All trademarks and brands within this book are for clarifying purposes only and are the owned by the owners themselves, not affiliated with this document.

Have Any Issues With This Book? Contact Randy at Randycfo@triggerhealthyhabits.com For Any Concerns About Quality, Copyright, Trademark, Or any issues or concerns you may have.

Your FREE Gift
Click Here

As a way of saying thank you,

Get your free natural therapeutic remedies report by clicking below.

What you'll receive

Enjoy the rest of the book!

Click here to get your Natural Therapeutic Remedies Report

The Benefits Of Short Reads,

Our Main Mission Is To Provide You With Quality Content In A Short Period Of Time, We Strive To Make Our Books Short And To The Point. These Days Who Has The Time To Read A Big Long Book? We Do Not Write Fiction Books, We Want To Help As Many People As Possible By Providing Them These Handbooks To Help Better Their Lives. We Hope You Enjoy This Kindle Short Reads E-Book

Table Of Contents

[Introduction](#)

[Why I Wrote This Book](#)

[What You Should Know Before Reading This Book](#)

[Tip 1 : Figure Out What Fits](#)

[Tip 2: Don't Get Too Set In Stone](#)

[Tip 3: It's Okay To Go Slow](#)

[Tip 4: Archways and Courtyards](#)

[Tip 5: PlantingTrees](#)

[Tip 6: The Benefit Of Hedgerows](#)

[Tip 7: Patchwork Gardens](#)

[Tip 8: Flowers](#)

[Conclusion](#)

Introduction

Have you been considering changing your yard? The same feel plain and boring to you? Don't worry, there are plenty of ways that you can make changes that will bring out the best in your garden. Decorating your yard and landscape is under wording, and will bring you pleasure for years and years afterward. Coming up with a design that makes you happy is a great way to make sure that you love your home and enjoy every minute to the fullest.

If changing your yard you want to do, following these simple to make sure that you do it as successfully as possible. This book will show you exactly what needs to be done in order to realize your full dream and enjoy your landscaping for years to come. It will show you the importance of staying true to yourself and your vision, while remaining flexible enough to work with your environment.

With this book, you will be able to do more with your space than you ever thought possible. So what are you waiting for? Let's start thinking about how to realize the potential of your dreams so that you too can have a great place to think, create, and be.

Why I Wrote This Book

This book because I know how important it is to enjoy nature, and a lot of people I to mediate by nature to venture much further than their own front yard. Fortunately, if your own front yard is a well landscaped, you will be more likely to go out and enjoy it. This book is full of great tips and advice on how to landscape your own yard and allow these beautiful and decorative ideas into your life.

If you want to enjoy well landscaped yard but never knew where to start, then this book is for you. I to empower people that they can enjoy every moment of their lives to the fullest. It's very important to be able to look outside your window and like what you see every single day. It will give you a great burst of satisfaction, and if you have a quiet and beautiful place to reflect, you will be happier and healthier in the long run. To me, that is worth every second of landscaping and I'd like to share it with you.

What You Need To Know Before Reading This Book

Before you read this book, you need to keep in mind that these projects can take quite a long time to come to fruition. Many people think that landscaping can happen overnight, and that is simply not true. Once you get your hands dirty, you'll find more and more things that need to be done, and this is common. It's actually part of the fun, it will give you a great chance to get to know your environment and what you want to get out of it.

You should be very careful if you are undergoing strenuous manual labor, and always have someone with you if it's a big job. That way, if you get hurt someone will be able to help you, and if you have a friend to help you out, it will be even more fun and rewarding. If you enjoy yourself while you're creating an enjoyable environment, you just can't go wrong. It will also help you to prevent injury, having somebody to help you do heavy lifting.

Remember to have fun and plan ahead, having the tools and knowledge ready to work with. Let it be a fun and life-changing projects, and just enjoy yourself.

Tip 1: Figure Out What Fits

Everybody has a different idea of what looks good. When it comes to landscaping, first thing you need to do is figure out what you think looks good to you. If you have to, drive around and examine other people's yards, thinking about what you do like and what you don't like and what you would like to see in your own yard. Many people landscape because it is aesthetically pleasing for other people, but you should think about what you like and what would bring you peace in your own home.

Notes on the like things you don't, and make a mental picture of what the yard would look like if you implemented these things into it. Make sure that you take into consideration when you would be using your yard the most, and what the weather is like during these times. If you are hoping to sit outside in the yard during the summer, you don't want to have your sitting area located directly in the sun when it is the hardest. Make sure you know your yard before planning out what to do.

Magazines for ideas and make sketches of the kinds of things that you want in your own yard. From there, you will be able to plan out exactly what you want to turn your yard from a boring, normal place into what could ultimately look like a fairytale garden full of magic and wonder. There are so many possibilities when it comes to landscaping, and taking great care of your yard will make you feel like a whole new person. Have fun with it and figure out exactly what you want!

Tip 2: Don't Get Too Set In Stone

Keep in mind when you are planning your landscaping is not to get your heart set on a specific outcome, as this can be dangerous for a few reasons. First of all, if you are simply thinking about when it comes to your yard and not about what it is actually like to sit in your yard, and you going to run into a few problems. If people are more comfortable sitting in one area then another, you should put the sitting area and there regardless of how it looks in your head. Be flexible and have fun, because sometimes nature and our plans aren't the same and won't work together very well.

It's important that you know your yard inside and out before you start making changes to it. You don't want to be that person who is making all the plans without even checking if they are feasible. It's great to dream big, but you also have to remain realistic. One of the best things to do before you make a large and permanent decision that will cost you a lot of money is to find out more about your yard by their and doing more outside just for relaxation's sake.

Think about the best area for your living things to be planted. Plants require certain amounts of sunlight, and each have their own specific needs comes to this. Be considerate of their needs so that they can thrive, and your yard will continue looking the best possible. Take long walks around your yard as you are formulating what you want in the long run. There is no better way to ensure satisfaction at the end of the day.

Tip 3: It's Okay To Go Slow

Many people think that landscaping is a quick job. How wrong I love you! Landscaping can take months of planning and even longer in execution. Sometimes it is a slow and steady process, and as you accumulate materials and resources, it slowly comes together into the yard of your dreams. This is actually a really good thing, because it means that you will appreciate your creation even more and have extra time to think about what you want. This will ensure satisfaction long term, the matter what might happen.

You don't have to be a superhero when it comes to getting everything in your yard finished. Although it will look wonderful when it's done, there is no deadline and the only person you have to please is yourself. If you are an overachiever, that's okay, just try to take a deep breath and allow yourself to relax and enjoy the process rather than urging onward toward completion.

You have to keep in mind, unless you are working with several other people, it's going to be very slow and arduous work. If you are doing all of it yourself or with the help of a few people and not the whole team, it's not going to happen quite as fast as you might be picturing it. It's still very hands-on and dirty work that takes a lot of muscle and time. This shouldn't be a problem, especially because it will give you more quality time with your yard so that you can figure out exactly what would be suited to it the best and where.

Tip 4: Archways and Courtyards

To luxury, most people think of yards that have courtyards and tremendous expansive gardens. That's no surprise, considering how relaxing it is to sit in a beautiful place and know that it is all your own. It is a true mark of success to be able to sit somewhere comfortable and read a book anytime you want to, or write out in nature. There is nothing more beautiful than that.

As far back as Emily Dickinson inspired deeply by these types of gardens, and creativity is just around the corner when you're in a beautiful yard. It's truly inspirational, and here are a few ways to ensure that your yard could also possess some of the great wonder and inspirational qualities of the beautiful landscaping.

Archways add an incredible effect to any yard, but especially one that is about landscaped and full of life. You can create an archway using plants themselves, or using wooden structures that will allow plans, like Ivy, to treat them and create a beautiful effect like a terrace. These add wonder and excitement to any scene, and would truly be a source of endless awe.

If you really want to go above and beyond, he could design your own courtyard. It may not be as difficult as it sounds, and a few things would make the courtyard come together. Stone paths and cobblestone courtyards are a great start. Benches on the cobblestone and having a fountain in the middle of it is truly magnificent. It's a great way to show how cultured you are and provide a peaceful and beautiful place for your creativity to shine or to simply relax and be part of nature.

Overall, the addition of any of these things is truly magnificent, and will add to the quality of your landscaping more than you could ever imagine.

Tip 5: Planting Trees

Another great way to add to your landscape is to plant trees. Trees out there, and trying to find the one that suits your yard the best can be both fun and challenging. Trees is a wonderful thing, and not only does it help to improve the quality of the air in the environment, but also provide shade, shelter, and beauty. They come in all shapes and sizes and colors, and if you wanted a great opportunity color and vivacious to your landscape, planting trees is the best idea.

Something that you can to add even more color and wonder to your garden to plant fruit trees. Fruit trees provide nourishment and plenty of snacks throughout the growing season, and if you are careful with your harvest, you can make all kinds of delicious things out of the fresh fruits and berries. Parties, juices, and all kinds of other desserts are on the horizon if you plan fruit trees in your yard. They will add so much color and character to your landscape that you won't even know where to begin looking.

Things that you can do with trees too, like creating a covered pathway with ministerial and magical quality to it like those in fairytales or in stories of ancient civilizations that adhered to the nature all around them. It's a very mystical and beautiful addition to any landscape, and planting trees not only helps to rid the world from the surplus of carbon dioxide in the atmosphere and decrease the greenhouse effect, but it will also provide you with fresh air and fresh fruit and berries for years to come, all free of charge.

Tip 6: The Benefit Of Hedgerows

Hedgerows are very popular in places like Ireland, where they are grown call people's prying eyes away from private land and also to provide structure for pathways where people walk. Hedgerows are bushes that grow tall and naturally, and can be sculpted to create a wall between you and whatever else you want. If you are looking for a great way to section off different areas of your yard and garden, the addition of hedgerows would be extremely beneficial.

They don't take a whole lot of maintenance, provide a beautiful addition to any yard or area in general, and function well as a way of keeping your privacy and creating a wall wherever you might want one. They have a very mystical quality about them, when one would assume would make a child want to play near them. You can create meetings with hedgerows or even a long, tall fence around your yard. There is no end you can do with hedgerows if you are creative.

Tip 7: Patchwork Gardens

So many different things that you can do with plants, and one of the most popular and beautiful as making patchwork gardens with them. Gardening is fun, but even more rewarding when it looks good too. If you want patchwork garden, it's very simple and very beautiful. All you have to do is get creative.

First of all, think about the plants that you want in your patchwork garden. This will help to lay out exactly where you want your garden to the. You can have these patchwork gardens sporadically throughout your lawn, using different types of plants even. If you wanted to make a patchwork garden, you would have to choose up to three different plants and have them alternate and box shape. For example, think of the checkerboard and imagine that every red and black space where a different type of flower. This works well with two different types of flowers or three or more, but it is more obvious when it's just two.

Simplicity can often speak volumes when it comes to landscaping, adding things like wild flowers that will constantly replenish themselves and take little pending can be fun and adventurous and add a nice burst of color and the landscape. Go ahead and get creative with your plants and the places that you choose to put these little gardens. If you don't like the idea of patchwork gardens, there are plenty of other things that you can do and you can look at other landscaping material for pictures to use as reference.

Tip 8: Flowers

When it comes to flowers during landscaping, they add an impressive charm that few other things possibly could. They're an incredible way to add color to an otherwise drab area and brighten things up so that they look as mystical and beautiful as possible. There are many ways that you can do this, including flowerbeds on the ground and in your windowsill.

Flowers can be arranged in many ways, and commonly are sorted by color and type. However, there are no rules for how you would like your flowers, so simply put them where you would like them the most and would benefit from them. They are a beautiful addition to any garden, and are guaranteed to make your day. They are versatile and easy to work with, all you have to do is find out where you want them and go from there.

Conclusion

Landscaping is a fine art, and one that can be utilized by anybody. All you have to do is have a fine eye for beauty and you will be able to find ways to make your yard look beautiful. Even if it's something as simple as putting rocks in the right place or planting flowers near your porch, landscaping is important and will provide an aesthetic that will please you for years to come.

Following the and advice in this book, you will be able to create the art of your dreams. Just remember to get to know your environment and figure out exactly what it is that you want. If you don't know what you're aiming for yet, don't worry about that. Just go ahead and take a look at other people's yards from the outside, up close if you've got permission, or look in landscaping books and magazines for pictures to help you visualize exactly what you're hoping for. From there, get to know your yard and figure out where everything would be best suited. You have the yard of your dreams in no time.

Although it takes years for the finished product to show up, the process itself is fun and exciting, and you should relish in the adventure. You can get things done fast with the large crew of people, you could take the time to do it slow and really get to know your yard and what you think would be best. All in all, you are creating a sanctuary for yourself, so take your time and do it right. Otherwise you might not enjoy the finished product quite as much. Don't waste all that time and money on something you don't feel connected to enough to use!

Now that you know what you do, go out there and get your hands dirty! Good luck! You can definitely do this.

Gardening

A Quick And Easy Guide To Efficiently Grow Organic Fruits And Vegetables In Your Backyard

Disclaimer
- Although the author and publisher have made every effort to ensure that the information in this book was correct at press time, the author and publisher do not assume and hereby disclaim any liability to any party for any loss, damage, or disruption caused by errors or omissions, whether such errors or omissions result from negligence, accident, or any other cause.
- This book is not intended as a substitute for the medical advice of physicians. The reader should regularly consult a physician in matters relating to his/her health and particularly with respect to any symptoms that may require diagnosis or medical attention.

Copyright 2014 by LOVE AND LIVE LIFE TO THE EXTREME FULLEST PUBLISHING- All rights reserved.

This document is geared towards providing exact and reliable information in regards to the topic and issue covered. The publication is sold with the idea that the publisher is not required to render accounting, officially permitted, or otherwise, qualified services. If advice is necessary, legal or professional, a practiced individual in the profession should be ordered.

- From a Declaration of Principles which was accepted and approved equally by a Committee of the American Bar Association and a Committee of Publishers and Associations.

In no way is it legal to reproduce, duplicate, or transmit any part of this document in either electronic means or in printed format. Recording of this publication is strictly prohibited and any storage of this document is not allowed unless with written permission from the publisher. All rights reserved.

The information provided herein is stated to be truthful and consistent, in that any liability, in terms of inattention or otherwise, by any usage or abuse of any policies, processes, or directions contained within is the solitary and utter responsibility of the recipient reader. Under no circumstances will any legal responsibility or blame be held against the publisher for any reparation, damages, or monetary loss due to the information herein, either directly or indirectly.

Respective authors own all copyrights not held by the publisher.

The information herein is offered for informational purposes solely, and is universal as so. The presentation of the information is without contract or any type of guarantee assurance.

The trademarks that are used are without any consent, and the publication of the trademark is without permission or backing by the trademark owner. All trademarks and brands within this book are for clarifying purposes only and are the owned by the owners themselves, not affiliated with this document.

Have Any Issues With This Book? Contact Randy at Randycfo@triggerhealthyhabits.com For Any Concerns About Quality, Copyright, Trademark, Or any issues or concerns you may have.

Your FREE Gift
Click Here

As a way of saying thank you,

Get your free natural therapeutic remedies report by clicking below.

What you'll receive

Enjoy the rest of the book!

Click here to get your Natural Therapeutic Remedies Report

The Benefits Of Short Reads,

Our Main Mission Is To Provide You With Quality Content In A Short Period Of Time, We Strive To Make Our Books Short And To The Point. These Days Who Has The Time To Read A Big Long Book? We Do Not Write Fiction Books, We Want To Help As Many People As Possible By Providing Them These Handbooks To Help Better Their Lives. We Hope You Enjoy This Kindle Short Reads E-Book

Table of Contents

[Introduction](#)
[Why Organic Farming?](#)
[Preparing to Plant](#)
[Plants, Plants, Plants](#)
[Watering and Weeding](#)
[Harvest Time!](#)
[Cleanup Time](#)
[Conclusion](#)

Introduction

Hello and thank you for checking out this book!

Organic gardening has recently started booming in many cases. It's a great way to grow your own food and know what you're getting out of it. For many, you might be a bit wary about organic gardening. You might think it's hard, or that it's a waste of time, or it might be better to just get everything from the store. But that might not be the case, because with organic gardening, you actually get what you want, when you want it, and you'll know exactly what you're getting when you do partake in organic farming. Many are turning to this, and not only is it good for you, it's a ton of fun as well.

The biggest question that you might have is, how do you start? How do you begin your adventure in organic farming? Well, the best way to do it is to read this book. This book will go through some of the amazing reasons why you should grow your own plants and vegetables, along with how to do it. The best part? It doesn't take a whole lot of skill to learn, and even those who don't have a green thumb can partake in organic farming and still get a lot out of it.

This is a beginner's guide to organic farming and how to go about it. Organic farming is simple, effective, and tasty as well. I wrote this book because I know that at first I was skeptical about it. I thought that organic farming was something only yuppie hippies do, and not something that directly affects me. But the truth is, it's not just for people like that anymore. It's a popularized way of gardening, and you should partake in it if you can. This book is a great guideline to starting the adventure of organic farming, and it's actually probably the best way to go about it. You don't have to be a scholar to understand it as well. You just have to know how to read, and you have to have a desire to learn new things. Doing just that will surely get you on the best pathway to growing your own vegetables. So what are you waiting for? It's time to get started on this, and your home life will never be the same again.

Why Organic Farming?

The first question you might ask yourself is why you would even do this. You might think that it's best to get things from the store and don't even bother with growing organic. Well the thing is, it's actually not the most ideal way to get food that you want, and it actually isn't as healthy as you think.

For one, think about many of the major food stores that sell organic that sell organic fruits and vegetables. Many of those foods are coming from all over the world, and it's obvious that there has to be a way to preserve it. It's actually not as natural as you think, and if you think about it, you're paying a lot for overpriced food that really isn't even that good for you. So who's really getting gypped here? You are. Don't be that person who think that stores like that are everything, because they're not.

Another benefit is that when you do grow organic, you decide what you're going to put on it. You can use natural insecticides, ones that are made naturally so they still don't hurt plants but also get rid of the nasty bugs. It is possible to use that, and many times foods from organic health food stores actually don't use that and end up using an insecticide that is permitted.

The FDA allows 20 different pesticides that are chemically-oriented on organic plants. That's right, there are still chemicals being sprayed on the food that you eat. Don't think you'll be escaping these as easy as you think if you choose to go through an organic food store instead of growing it on your own.

However, with organic you can control what you use. It's also a whole lot cheaper in the grand scheme of things. Many of those foods you buy from the store are filled with chemicals, just like non-organic food. So you're being duped in many cases, but if you buy organic, you're the real winner at the end of the day.

Plus, there is a feeling of self-satisfaction when you grow your own plants. It tastes fresher better, and it's not bad for you. You made it in a sense, so it gives you that sense of pride that you don't get from buying at the store. It's another benefit about growing organically. Plus, it's a great skill set to have. You can grow your own food, and you can even teach your family and progeny about how to grow like this. It's a fresher way to grow your own food, and you'll feel great about it.

Growing organic has a bit of a leverage against just buying things at the store. The only drawback is it takes a bit long, but the rewards are worth it at the end. You'll learn all about the different ways to grow some of the great foods that you love, and at the end of the day, it's worth it to really get the result that you want out of your garden, and the feelings that you've always wanted from growing your own food.

Preparing to Plant

The first thing to go over is preparing to plant. Now, you first want to choose a place for your garden. Ideally, choose a place that has ample sunlight for sun plants, and also some shade for those that grow in the shade. You want to make sure that the soil is properly cared for an organic garden so that your plants can grow stronger plants. You can test the soil by getting a home testing kit. You can look at the pH and nutrient levels and see if it's possible to grow organic there. You can ten tailor the soil to your best specifications, and from that, you can grow whatever you want there. You should ideally do this in the fall and winter to predetermine where to plant things.

If you're pressed for time, you can also mix put a mixtures inside the soil. To do this, you just mix in some compost, grass, and manure into the area designated. When you're looking for manure, get it from local and organic farmers, and ideally get it from ones that don't eat meat. It's full of more nutrients, and you'll get more out of this. Make sure to do this first before you plant anything, because healthy soil is the only way to really get results with this.

Then there is compost. You should start to build a compost at this point, as it is the ideal way to get the plants that you want. Compost is very important for organic plants, because it helps conserve water, cuts down weed production, and it keeps waste out of landfills. It's a great way to help lower the carbon footprint you leave on the planet as well, and it helps you grow plants so much better.

For the best results, you're going to want a ratio of air, soil and water that is equal so that the nitrogen and carbon are balanced out. It sounds weird and it might make you think like you really do need a rocket scientist to grow this sort of thing, but truth be told, it's very simple.

To do this, get a 3x3 space ready for your compost heap. Once you do that, start adding in the mixture for the compost, starting with carbon material, such as leaves and grass, and then nitrogen material, which for example is leftover food. You then put soil in between there. Once you're done, at the top of the pile you put about 4-6 inches of soil. You can then turn the pile to mix the layers and add in a little bit of water to start microbial action in the soil. This is the best way to help you generate the soil that you want easily, and without any problems whatsoever.

Plants, Plants, Plants

Now comes the fun part. That is choosing the right plants. Now, the first thing you'll probably think is you have to pick all of your favorite plants, but the thing is you have to mix them in the right way so that you get the results you want. You will want to pick plants that are good for the atmospheres you're about to subject them to. Look at where you live and the ideal growing conditions for the plants. If your area fits it, then you'll be good to go. You should also look for plants that grow best where you live. Don't get plants that grow in tropical locales if you live in a cool and dry place. That will set you up for failure. Usually, you can check online for the hardness zones for the best results, which is usually updated every Arbor day for your convenience.

Also choose plants that can be fitted for the location that you put them in, especially with regards to how much light and water the plant gets, and even based off the health of the soil. Soil is different in many places, and if you put them in the right locations, they will be less susceptible to dying, which is very important.

To start, pick plants that grow from a seed so you can get used to it. Many examples of this are sunflowers, poppies, larkspur, morning glories, squash, peas, and cucumbers. These plants are easy to grow, and if you want, you'll get some great results from this.

You can also build beds for some plants. Strawberries grow well, but you'll have to build a wooden bed first. The reason is because they grow on the ground and they have tendrils that go everywhere, so it's best to keep them contained in one area. Doing this will help you maintain control over your plants, and it will make things all the more easier.

Now, when it comes to harvesting plants, such as vegetables and flowers that you might cut, you should grow them together in beds that are there just to hold the plants. Don't walk on these, but rather keep them off to the side. You can put them in raised beds to help with this. The reason why you group them is because it reduces weeding, waste, and it helps get more nutrients to them. Plus it's way easier going to one area to pick your carrots than having to go all over your garden just to find them. It also helps you keep the path and soil better and reduces fungal attacks.

You should make sure that you give ample space to all your plants. It may look tiny now, but looks are deceiving, and many times plants grow to become way larger than you expect, so read the packets and choose the locations carefully.

Watering and Weeding

Next comes the proper maintenance of plants, which is just as important as everything else. For starts, you will have to water and weed your plants. Sounds hard? Well, it's how you take care of these plants, and you have to do it to help keep your organic plants safe from harm. Also, water is how plants make their food, so you need to water.

Ideally, plants should be watered early in the morning. You will lose less water during then, and it will allow the plants to soak up what they need and let it evaporate at night. If you water at night, the plants will likely stay damp, and sometimes this leads to fungal pathogens on the plants, which can kill them.

When watering, you should water the roots, and not the greenery and flowers. This can get right down to the base, and it will let the plant soak it up. For many that are already established, you should water them infrequently, but substantially, which is usually an inch or so. If it's not wet outside, apply it to the plants twice a week to promote better rooting and stronger plants. You should use water at near air temperature so that it soaks up faster as well, which will make your plants thrive all the more better. Ideally, watch the plants and test the soil to see how much water they really need.

For weeding, the best thing to do is apply mulch. This helps protect the soil, and organic mulch will also protect the soil and will look better. You can also use burlap as well for vegetables and fruits. You can do wood chips as well, but that can get pricy, and it's not the best. You can also use lawn clippings to help with weeds too.

For insects and other such predators, use flowery plants with blossoms to attract them so they don't hurt the others. The thing is, if you don't use some type of insecticide, you can potentially hurt the plant. But, if you want there are different organic means to spray the plants to protect them from bugs. Look for an organic insecticide that won't hurt plants and will keep the nasty predators away.

Harvest Time!

Now comes the benefits of your labor, which is harvesting your precious fruits. There are a few things to keep in mind however in order to get the best response. Use these tips to help you get your plants out of the soil in the best ways possible and without hurting any of the plants.

To start, do so in the fall season. That's when most plants are ready. Start with the herbs, for they're the easiest to get out. It's best to get as much as you can as soon as it starts to sprout, unless you plan on drying them, which in that case wait for them to flower. That's when it's best to get them. If you have basil, harvest that in the late afternoon.

For leafy greens, don't take all of it out at once, but a little at a time. If you have to harvest some broccoli, check to see that the head is fully grown and healthy before you get to cutting it. If you get it above where the leaves are then you will get way more as time goes on from that same plant. Use a knife or scissors because it will prevent damage to the plant so more can grow from it. If you have too much, the best thing to do is to put some away to freeze and then have it later.

If you have fruits, grab them from the stem and cut off. Don't pull it because it can damage the plant. Be chary while doing this, and you will get more from your plants than ever before. You should check them every day too, base you'll never know what you're going to get.

Cleanup Time

Now you've reached either the end of the season or year. Or you might just have a lot of plants that ae not surviving. For many first-time growers, the latter might be the biggest problem. However, there is a way to clean it up without hurting the other plants. If you're going to clean up, here are some tips on how to do it.

Take the whole plant away and don't forget to grab anything underneath. The reasoning for this is because diseased leaves can cause microbes to get into your other plants, which isn't good. If you have any infected material, toss it in the woods near your home, and make sure if you do bury it on the same land that you bury it deep so it won't affect your plants. You can also scrap them in a fire, or bury them, but they must be at least a foot deep.

For the survivors, you can just cover them from the elements when you're done, and you can protect them from any birds or other predators. Ideally, many of the annual plants should be cleaned up, so do away with them like how it's said above. But keep the perineals intact unless they're infected, for they will continue to grow regardless, and you'll have more plants for now, and in the future. Growing plants can be fun, and the ones that do survive will be ready to continue flowering and living next year.

Conclusion

Thanks for checking out this book!

Growing plants might seem hard, but I hope this book taught you a thing or two about it. It's actually a whole lot of fun, and you can learn a lot from it. Growing plants isn't some sort of rocket science, but rather, it's a means to grow things that you want, and it will help you build an organic garden that you desire. Organic gardens are great, and you should partake in them as needed. It's a skill that anyone can learn regardless of who you are, and you can then have a great organic garden in no time. Your entire family can get into it as well, and soon you will have an amazing garden that you and your family can be both proud of and excited to work on in many different ways and in many different cases.

The next thing you should do is start your organic garden. If it's late into the season already, prepare for next year, but if it's peak time, get ready and start to prepare your organic garden for the plants that you want. Starting it now will yield great results, and I can assure you that you'll be happy with the fruits and vegetables that you produce. Happy gardening!

Greenhouse Gardening

How To Effectively Grow Fruits, Vegetables, And Plants All Year In A Greenhouse Efficiently

Disclaimer
- Although the author and publisher have made every effort to ensure that the information in this book was correct at press time, the author and publisher do not assume and hereby disclaim any liability to any party for any loss, damage, or disruption caused by errors or omissions, whether such errors or omissions result from negligence, accident, or any other cause.
- This book is not intended as a substitute for the medical advice of physicians. The reader should regularly consult a physician in matters relating to his/her health and particularly with respect to any symptoms that may require diagnosis or medical attention.

Copyright 2014 by LOVE AND LIVE LIFE TO THE EXTREME FULLEST PUBLISHING- All rights reserved.

This document is geared towards providing exact and reliable information in regards to the topic and issue covered. The publication is sold with the idea that the publisher is not required to render accounting, officially permitted, or otherwise, qualified services. If advice is necessary, legal or professional, a practiced individual in the profession should be ordered.

- From a Declaration of Principles which was accepted and approved equally by a Committee of the American Bar Association and a Committee of Publishers and Associations.

In no way is it legal to reproduce, duplicate, or transmit any part of this document in either electronic means or in printed format. Recording of this publication is strictly prohibited and any storage of this document is not allowed unless with written permission from the publisher. All rights reserved.

The information provided herein is stated to be truthful and consistent, in that any liability, in terms of inattention or otherwise, by any usage or abuse of any policies, processes, or directions contained within is the solitary and utter responsibility of the recipient reader. Under no circumstances will any legal responsibility or blame be held against the publisher for any reparation, damages, or monetary loss due to the information herein, either directly or indirectly.

Respective authors own all copyrights not held by the publisher.

The information herein is offered for informational purposes solely, and is universal as so. The presentation of the information is without contract or any type of guarantee assurance.

The trademarks that are used are without any consent, and the publication of the trademark is without permission or backing by the trademark owner. All trademarks and brands within this book are for clarifying purposes only and are the owned by the owners themselves, not affiliated with this document.

Have Any Issues With This Book? Contact Randy at Randycfo@triggerhealthyhabits.com For Any Concerns About Quality, Copyright, Trademark, Or any issues or concerns you may have.

Your FREE Gift
Click Here

As a way of saying thank you,

Get your free natural therapeutic remedies report by clicking below.

What you'll receive

Enjoy the rest of the book!

Click here to get your Natural Therapeutic Remedies Report

The Benefits Of Short Reads,

Our Main Mission Is To Provide You With Quality Content In A Short Period Of Time, We Strive To Make Our Books Short And To The Point. These Days Who Has The Time To Read A Big Long Book? We Do Not Write Fiction Books, We Want To Help As Many People As Possible By Providing Them These Handbooks To Help Better Their Lives. We Hope You Enjoy This Kindle Short Reads E-Book

Table of Contents

Introduction 56
Getting Started with the Greenhouse 57
Extending the growing season 59
Furnishing your Greenhouse 60
Deciding the Plants 62
Lighting 63
Conclusion 64

Introduction

Hello and thank you for checking out this book

Greenhouse gardening. Its type of gardening that you can do all year around, and it's something that many are interested in. You need to have a lot of discipline in order to do this, but it's possible. It's a lot of fun as well, and with this, you can grow your own vegetables in an effective manner, and without too much trouble. But for many, it might be a struggle because of what you have to do initially. There is a lot that goes into this, and for some, it might be overwhelming. However, this book will help you out with it, for it is the answer to the question of "how do I start greenhouse gardening?" Greenhouse gardening might seem scary, but this book is going to help you get on the right path.

I have been tending to a greenhouse for a while, and I know some helpful tips and tricks on how to go about this. This book will give you a good understanding on how to start, what to do, and where to go with this. From this, you'll go from not being able to start a greenhouse, to having your own. It's simple and fun, and you'll learn many new things. Greenhouse gardening will allow you to have the plants that you want at any time of the year, and it's cheap too. You will also get the benefit of earing fresh plants right from your home. You're about to go on an adventure, and I hope you'll be able to create the greenhouse of your dreams from this. It will instruct you on how to go about it, and by the end of it you'll be able to do so in no time. Have fun!

Getting Started with the Greenhouse

The first thing to do is to figure out how to get started. The main question is how you're going to build this. For many, you might start off with recyclable materials, because it's insanely cheaper than having someone come out and build you a greenhouse. However, if you're not a handy person, you'll want to build it yourself. Also, recycling materials might be good, but in the long run it might not be. For example, polyethylene film is cheap, but it ages and has to be replaced every three months. Shop around for materials that work well. Ideally, go with fiberglass and panels of plastics for this because it's almost shatterproof and it's inexpensive. For you, it's best to get a guy out there to build it for you, but tell them that the roof needs to be made of fiberglass.

Then there is the aspect of attached or freestanding. Attached greenhouses are attached to something such as the main house, and it has more strength. You can also add the water and heating to this. It's easier to maintain, and it loses less heat faster. You can also use an attached on as a sitting room, however it might be what you want, so think twice about this.

You can get a self-supporting one, but it will cost more, and you'll have to attach water and heat to this. For some, it might not be the most ideal, but for many it might give the greenhouse better light. However, make sure that it's attached to the ground, for if it's not, it could blow away with the wind or be damaged due to the weather.

When choosing a space, pick a spot that is able to get the most sunlight. Watch out for trees and buildings as well, for even ones far away might be shaded. Also, check with your town for zoning restrictions as well, and make sure that you do this before you begin construction so you're able to save a lot of time.

It's important as well to take wind into consideration. It might not be able to trap sun in some locations, but might be better in others. Also, include a place that allows drainage. The drainage can definitely pile up, and that creates a situation that you don't need. So think about these two things before you put your greenhouse in.

Finally, make sure that you're able to get electricity out to it. It creates quite a problem if you're not able to, because during the winter you might need to get heat lamps installed to help with growth, and you'll need to maintain the greenhouse at the correct temperature. It's in your best interest to make sure that it's in a space where you can get electricity, because it's a key factor in aiding the growth of your plants.

Next, you can build it. The best thing to do is to get someone to build it for you. If you're not the handy type, and especially since this is your first greenhouse, it's in your best interest not to take it upon yourself to do this. It's better if you let someone else do it, because it will be built by someone with experience and t's less liable to get wrecked.

All of these are factors that you need to keep in mind when you're building a greenhouse. It's how you get started, but make sure that you follow everything so that it's done in a correct and effective manner.

Extending the growing season

Now that everything is up, it's time to talk about how to extend the growing season before you get started. For many, the first thing you might think of is the amount of plants you can grow. But, you also have to remember that you might get plants that are off-season, and it's hard to maintain those. However, there is a way to grow plants year-round and to keep the off-season vegetables growing and producing what it needs to produce. You can do this easily, but make sure that you follow everything.

The first thing is heat. You have to keep things at a high temperature. Frost is a way many plants die, so you have to insulate and keep the temperature in the greenhouse at a good level. You might also need a humidifier as well, simply because when it gets colder you will notice that the air gets drier, making it harder for water to get into the plants so they can create food. Watch for this, and make sure that it's warm.

Another thing to do is to install sun lamps. These lamps will shine on the plants and will help them produce chlorophyll, which is their food. Plants need the sun in order to generate food, but during the off-season, it can be hard for them to germinate simply because of the lack of sunlight. Keep them on for a while, and you'll be able to help the plants grow to where they need to get to.

Make sure as well to plant them in the correct time. Plant them as soon as possible, and make sure that there is enough crop to be harvested by mid-October. During the winter, the plants will grow at a slow rate, and for some plants, the lights might not work. Make sure to harvest during then and maintain the plants to keep them going, for that will let them live longer.

Also, check the water as well. Due to the slower nature of growing during the off-season, some plants might not need as much water. Examine the dirt and stick your finger in it to determine, and also watch for any potential yellowing of plants. Yellowing of plant leaves means that it's getting too much water, and it can die from that, so be chary about that.

For frost, the best way to cover plants is to either use blankets, or floating row covers. A blanket is great as long as the fabric is dry. In a greenhouse, normally these can be used to help keep it warm. The floating row covers are fabrics that can be used over crops. It also transmits light, so it can extend crop protection, along with making sure that it screen s them from insects. These are the best to use if you choose to cover your plants in the greenhouse.

Extending the plant life might be hard for some, but if you're able to do this, it will keep them alive for longer.

Furnishing your Greenhouse

Next comes the furnishings, which are very important. You have to make sure you're getting the most out of your benches and space, and this section will talk about the best ways to go about this in your greenhouse.

The first thing to do, is to think like you're playing Tetris. That's right, think about how you can put as many plants as possible in there, while still making sure everyone gets sunlight. Stacking plants on top of one another is not ideal, but building shelves to house plants so that they can get light and so you can have more light are definitely important.

For benches, don't make these benches wider than three feet. For one, it will make it hard for you to get the plants in the back, and you won't be able to get as much water there. Also make sure that your planters are at least six inches deep to get some water. Leave a little space to get the drainage for the plants while still keeping the humidity and space cleared.

Next is flooring. You should use concrete for this because for one, it's strong and you won't slip on it from all the water being drained. You can also use plain dirt covered with gravel or rocks as well to help absorb the water. However, avoid linoleum or wood floors. For one, they're prone to being slick so you might slip and fall, and plus they de-humidify the air, which isn't what you want. That will dry out the plants in the building, something you definitely don't need.

For a greenhouse, make sure you have a corner designated for potting. You should create a storage space in the corner for tools and supplies. There should also be a space as well for potting and repotting plants, and there also should be a place to prune and clean up your plants if any leaves start to dry up and die. However, this isn't a huge thing that's needed, but rather an extra attachment that will help you when you're in your greenhouse. Don't make it too huge, because it's not necessary. Make it so that it's enough room for you to work with one plant, and ideally do it in the corner of the greenhouse. You can also attach a shed to do this in if you so desire, and if possible, put a wink in for cleanup.

When it comes to water, put in water lines pretty much everywhere. Do this before you put in the walls, walkways, and floor. You should also put in tanks for rainwater if possible, and make sure that there is enough places so that you can put it all over the place. Ideally, irrigation systems that water the plants naturally are your best bet, and it's the best way to water everything without too much work.

Then there are glass shelves that allow you to place plants where you want to put them in order to grow more in the space that you have. You can put these all over the place to extend the growing room. Also hanging pots can get sunlight as well as long as they're not directly over any plants. You can put these pretty much anywhere that gets light and soon your plants will be able to grow there as well.

And finally, give a bit of space to places under benches. You might think it's odd to have a space under benches, but for some plants, it's actually better for them. If you're planning on growing any plants that do well in the shade, then this is imperative. Installing this will improve your plant's life, and it will make things easier on these plants.

Installing furniture in a greenhouse can be exhausting, but doing so will allow you to create a space that you want without too much trouble. Create the greenhouse that you want, and you'll have t up and running in no time.

Deciding the Plants

Next comes the fun part, which is deciding where the plants go. This might seem kind of small, but it's very important. You should make sure you planet everything in the correct location, because doing so can make or break a garden. This section will go over some of the best ways to help you determine the plants you're going to grow, along with how to handle this in the greenhouse.

For starters, divide the plants by seasons and plant accordingly. You should make sure that you know where some of these plants grow best, such as shade or sun. Study the packets, and also look at the temperatures dictated on them. If they're the type that can survive cooler seasons, wait until late summer to plant. But if they're summer plants, plant at the correct time. Not every plant is the same you know.

Along with that, you need to make sure that the greenhouse is the correct climate for each of these. For many, they erratically put everything in one place and call it that. The thing is, plants need different levels of humidity and temperatures, and some need more humidity to accomplish growth. You can divide the greenhouse by different types and maintain the environment, however that might be a bit hard and it can end up being very expensive. The best way to go about this is to actually determine which season you're planting what, and when it's planted make sure the plants are similar. If you can, designate an area that is less humid for humid-sensitive plants, and for those that need a ton of humidity, place them in apt locations. Also adding a bit of water to ones that need humidity can do the trick as well. Also watching for warm plants and cold plants is important too.

Plants are different, just like people are, and you need to plant each of these plants accordingly based on their needs. Doing so will allow you to have the greenhouse garden of your dreams, and it will make your job all the more easier.

Lighting

Finally, there is lighting. Lighting is super important for plants because that is how they make their food. However, there are some lights that you can use, and you want to make sure that you get the right things. Many don't realize that you have to choose the right lights for a plant, and using just any old light won't work. You can't just use an incandescent bulb because it won't grow as well, but there are different lights you can get.

The first type is a plant light. These will help the plant grow, and they can be helpful. You can get these at any hardware store for cheap, and they definitely do the trick.

Then there are growing lights, which can be used in the winter season. They work for plants that are cold-weather plants mostly, so make sure that you're using it on plants like that to help extend the growing season. However, for those that need more light, it won't work well, so be wary and choose wisely which plants are going to work.

Then there is solar lighting. This is great for greenhouses that are in direct sunlight, for it can help you get natural lighting in there without too much trouble. The best thing to do is to build the panels near a brick wall, and then use the lighting within the greenhouse later on. Solar lighting panels can also be installed on the greenhouse as well, but make sure that you're not blocking any of the plants from getting light. It's a great, natural way to help you get light however.

Lighting is very important, so it's in your best interest to invest wisely in it. Doing so will allow you to have a better gardening experience, and it will allow you to grow plants that look great, and ones that produce a lot.

Conclusion

Thank you again for downloading this book!

I hope I was able to help you learn a lot about how to create a greenhouse garden. Greenhouse gardens are a ton of fun to make, and they definitely do a lot for a person. A greenhouse will allow you to cultivate and make the plants that you want to make, and you'll be able to do so with this book. This book walked you through some of the major points in building a greenhouse, and some of the important things you must keep in mind in order to be successful in greenhouse gardening.

Your next step is to actually start building one. However, you need to make sure that you choose the correct locations, places to go, and where the best lighting is to help your plants grow. Take some time and put some thought into this, and it will help you determine what to do. Greenhouse gardening is very important is you want to create your own plants, and if you're a gardener with a green thumb, it's also a ton of fun to do. But it's time to get started, and by doing so, you'll be able to create the greenhouse of your dreams. It's time for you to get started, so do so right away and cultivate some amazing plants that you will definitely enjoy.

Grow Fruit Indoors

How To Grow Fruit Indoors To Have A Sustainable Source Of Fruits All Year Round!

Disclaimer
- Although the author and publisher have made every effort to ensure that the information in this book was correct at press time, the author and publisher do not assume and hereby disclaim any liability to any party for any loss, damage, or disruption caused by errors or omissions, whether such errors or omissions result from negligence, accident, or any other cause.
- This book is not intended as a substitute for the medical advice of physicians. The reader should regularly consult a physician in matters relating to his/her health and particularly with respect to any symptoms that may require diagnosis or medical attention.

Copyright 2014 by LOVE AND LIVE LIFE TO THE EXTREME FULLEST PUBLISHING- All rights reserved.

This document is geared towards providing exact and reliable information in regards to the topic and issue covered. The publication is sold with the idea that the publisher is not required to render accounting, officially permitted, or otherwise, qualified services. If advice is necessary, legal or professional, a practiced individual in the profession should be ordered.

- From a Declaration of Principles which was accepted and approved equally by a Committee of the American Bar Association and a Committee of Publishers and Associations.

In no way is it legal to reproduce, duplicate, or transmit any part of this document in either electronic means or in printed format. Recording of this publication is strictly prohibited and any storage of this document is not allowed unless with written permission from the publisher. All rights reserved.

The information provided herein is stated to be truthful and consistent, in that any liability, in terms of inattention or otherwise, by any usage or abuse of any policies, processes, or directions contained within is the solitary and utter responsibility of the recipient reader. Under no circumstances will any legal responsibility or blame be held against the publisher for any reparation, damages, or monetary loss due to the information herein, either directly or indirectly.

Respective authors own all copyrights not held by the publisher.

The information herein is offered for informational purposes solely, and is universal as so. The presentation of the information is without contract or any type of guarantee assurance.

The trademarks that are used are without any consent, and the publication of the trademark is without permission or backing by the trademark owner. All trademarks and brands within this book are for clarifying purposes only and are the owned by the owners themselves, not affiliated with this document.

Have Any Issues With This Book? Contact Randy at Randycfo@triggerhealthyhabits.com For Any Concerns About Quality, Copyright, Trademark, Or any issues or concerns you may have.

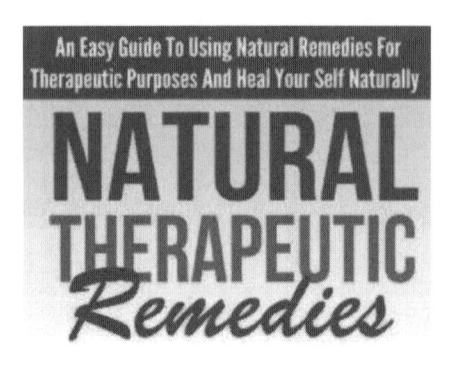

Your FREE Gift
Click Here

As a way of saying thank you,

Get your free natural therapeutic remedies report by clicking below.

What you'll receive

Enjoy the rest of the book!

Click here to get your Natural Therapeutic Remedies Report

The Benefits Of Short Reads,

Our Main Mission Is To Provide You With Quality Content In A Short Period Of Time, We Strive To Make Our Books Short And To The Point. These Days Who Has The Time To Read A Big Long Book? We Do Not Write Fiction Books, We Want To Help As Many People As Possible By Providing Them These Handbooks To Help Better Their Lives. We Hope You Enjoy This Kindle Short Reads E-Book

Table of Contents

Introduction 71

What you Need 72

The Best Seeds 73

Time to Plant! 74

Light for Plants... 75

Transplanting Plants 76

Extra Tidbits 77

Conclusion 78

Introduction

Hello and thank you for checking out this book!

Many times, you want to grow some of your favorite foods and you want to have them all year round. You might even have a garden planted, and it might be doing great. But for some, they want to get their food all year round from a garden, and that requires a bit of work. You can grow fruit indoors, but it's a bit hard for some. However, this book will make that dream of being able to, a reality.

It actually can be done in a few simple steps. It takes a bit of preparation for the seeds and such, and it might be best if you take your time and only grow a few things at first, but you can practically grow anything you like with this simple guide to growing fruit indoors, and it's something that many people need to indulge in. It's actually pretty simple once you get the hang of it, and if you take plants from outside and bring them in, it's definitely possible.

When growing fruit indoors, you have to keep a few things in mind. That's why this book was written, to help you keep some of the essential points in mind before you go on your adventure into growing fruits indoors. You can also grow organically in this way as well, it just takes a little bit of time and effort, and you might have to practice a little bit. But growing fruit indoors is totally possible, and this book will show you how.

I wrote this book because I feel like people should know how to grow fruit indoors. It's actually very simple, and I myself was as bit wary at first. I mean after all, it seems too good to be true, and you might be a bit worried about some of the constraints attached to it. But, if you know about the different steps that you must take, you'll be fine. You have to do a little bit of preparation first, and once you know how to go about it, the rest of it is cake.

It's time to grow the fruit that you want indoors, so you can have it all year round. You can still have a great supply of fruits even in the winter time, and this book will go over how to do so, and how to grow some of the plants that you love without sacrificing anything in order to do so.

What you Need

The first thing that any person who wants to grow food indoors should do, is to get the materials you need. This chapter will highlight some of the important things you must have in order to grow fruit indoors, and any preparation that you will have to do.

The first thing is a location. Location is essential to growing fruit indoors, especially if you live in a place where the climate goes from being very warm to very cold. If the temperatures flip flop like crazy, that also needs to be taken into consideration. Ideally, pick a place that keeps at a very nice temperature, around 70-80 degrees. You will want to pick a place that also allows a bunch of sunlight to come on through. During the winter, you'll be getting less sunlight, so you have to make do with what you got. You should ideally try to put it in a place that will have sunlight directly on it, and if it's a shaded plant, keep it nearby as well. Just because it says shade during the summer doesn't mean that keeping it in the dark will make it grow. You won't get a proper fruit from it because the sunlight is not as strong during the summer and it's out for less time. So be careful with this because it actually can affect the plant.

Once you have a location, get some boxes to place the plants in if you're growing a fruit that's usually in a raised bed. You should also get some organic soil as well, and it will help bring nutrients to the soil. Ideally, you should get some plant food too so that it grows even better than before. You need to watch out for this, because if you don't have a good eye on the plants, they won't grow.

Next you should also invest in some pots for plants that climb. It's the best location for them, such as if you're growing something with a vine on it. Get that, along with a trellis and start to put it in a place that gets sunlight. Doing so will get your plant you grow in no time, and it will climb instead of spread out all over the floor.

Now that you have everything to start, it's time to go over the next part, which is seeds and the different types. That will be talked about in the next chapter in greater detail, spirally the types of seeds you should get for this endeavor.

The Best Seeds

When growing plants indoors, the best thing to do is to pick the right seeds for the situation. For many, the right seed can determine whether or not you're going to get a crop out of that batch of plants. Its' imperative to know about the types of seeds you're getting, and to choose wisely. This chapter will be going over the best seeds to get, and what kinds you should get to grow indoors well.

Now, you might think that the first thing you should get is the ones that you like. That might work, but many plants are tropical, and they won't do well at all in most climates that get blow 70 degrees. Even a tiny bit of cold could kill those plants, so go for something more durable. Ideally, tomatoes and peas are your best bet, as they are easy to grow, and they are durable once they've sprouted. For people starting in this endeavor, tomatoes are your best option.

Now, you should also look and see when they got to be planted. If they're the type of plant that needs some time to germinate, and you're already into the fall season, it's best not to use that. You probably want something that can germinate fast so that you can get it started before the growing season is done. There are a lot of options, but get them fast.

Another way to get seeds is to go to your local organic farmer and purchase them. These seeds are usually better than their store counterparts are because normally they are just taken, so they're full of nutrients. You should get seeds of plants that grow fast and ripen very fast. You can also get ones that are fitting to your location as well. If you don't want to stack plants, such as in the case of strawberries, go with something that takes up less space and volume. It will definitely be easier if you have that, because it will reduce the size of your indoor garden. You should go with something a bit small at first too in order to get used to it, such as cherry tomatoes, because they are easier to keep under control indoors, and you'll be able to get more out of it.

Growing fruit indoors seems hard, but determining the right seed is essential. It's what your plant is going to be coming out of, and you need the best to get the results that you want, and from this, you'll end up with a much better result in no time.

Time to Plant!

Now it's time for the fun part, which is planting seeds. It takes a bit at first, but if you do this well and correctly, you'll have plants in no time. You want to be careful with this, because if you don't follow instructions, they won't grow. You should first make sure that you have the materials that you need before starting.

You should have most things by now, such as soil, seed, fertilizer, some containers to put everything in, and an ample space. Make sure that you purchase a lot of this, and ideally start a bit earlier than the end of the growing season. The reasoning for this is because it will get you familiar with how to grow fruit indoors before you start to take on the harsher months. You should try by around august or September to start off.

To begin, get your containers or area properly filled with soil and have little holes dug in them for the seed. Grab your seed, and put a couple inside each container. You should put them about ¼-1 inch deep, depending on what your seed packet says. Some might need to be deeper, some shallower. You should also give it a bit of water, and make sure that the soil is also of room temperature. You should then place them near the window in order to allow them to germinate, and you should add a little bit of fertilizer in them. Ideally, keep them at room temperature, and don't let them dry out. You can also place them in various locations depending upon where the sun is. But be careful, because sometimes too much sun can dry out.

You need to check the plants when you do take care of them. Check for their water, and if they're dry, do the plants a favor and water them. However, make sure that you don't water them too much, for they might get oversaturated, and a fungus grows on plants when they're like that. It's not ideal for any plant to be like that, so just be wary. Watch your plants, and when they're ready, you can then move onto the next step, which is harvesting. When that's ready, just cut them at the right level without hurting the plant, and then you have some fruit. Now that you know the basics, it's time to go into detail on a couple of other little points that are of great importance to a plant.

Light for Plants

There is a part of growing plants that many people seem to forget. That is the concept of light, and the fact that it's very important for a plant. Light is essential for any plant out there, after all that's how they make their food and it's how they grow. Having ample light for any plant is essential, but there are some things you have to keep in mind. For one, some plants don't get enough light in the winter, especially when they days start getting shorter. This could cause them to starve and die, and that's not good at all. However, this chapter will go over how to take care of a plant when it's cold, and how to give it ample light.

The best thing to do is to watch the sun. As soon as it's up, place the plants out there. You might then have to play the fun game of turning the plants when needed. This will let the light bask on them in various areas, and it's essential for any plant to live. You might have to do this a few times a day, but it's a great and inexpensive way to help your plants get the light that they need.

There is another option as well, which is buying plant food. Plant food can be given to any plant to help it germinate and grow, and it can be a good way to help a plant reach peak levels. Fertilizer along with this is a great way to get the plant growing, and it's not too expensive and will help a plant reach its harvest level.

Finally, there is the concept of a heat lamp. A heat lamp is very important for a plant as well, and you will want to keep one nearby. They can be expensive, but they are a great substitute for sunlight during the harsh winter months. You'll probably only need one or two to start off, and you can put the light over the plant when it needs it. They will allow the plant to soak it up, make food, and thereby live a bit longer. It's a last resort, but it's something important that anyone should know if they're going to grow fruit indoors.

Transplanting Plants

Now, you can take a plant from outside and put it inside, but it does take a little bit of work. You should be careful with this though, because this puts the plant at great risks and it can make sprouting and letting the roots sink into the soil a lot harder, and you're risking losing the plant. You should be careful with this, but it can be done. The steps are in this section of the book.

The first thing to do is to pick a plant that isn't super old, but not one that is a baby as well. Make sure it has enough time to sprout and develop a bit, and you can then use it. Ideally, if you have one from this growing season that you want to take into the winter months, use that.

Once you've chosen your plant, dig it up, but be careful with the roots. Grab it from the very ends and pull it out, clipping if necessary. Don't take any part of the root too close to the plant because that could risk losing everything. So be careful with this.

Once you do that, get the transplant container and put a hole in it. Place the plant in, and make sure that you have enough soil around it, along with ample fertilizer and plant food. This will make the plant get the nutrients it needs, and if you have organic, natural compost in the plant, it will definitely have a better chance of living

Water this plant thoroughly, and make sure that it germinates in ample time. It might take a bit, but if you watch it like a hawk and take care of it, it will germinate into the plant that you want. Doing this takes time, but if you're careful, you will get a plant that you desire.

Extra Tidbits

There are a few things to keep in mind when you're growing plants, and this chapter will go over it. These extra parts of it are very important, and you need to know about them in order to get seeds to sprout and germinate. This chapter will go over some of the important maintenance things to keep in mind so you can have good, healthy plants.

The first thing is get a humidifier. Many plants need that, especially during the winter months. Winter is cold and dry, and even though you might be able to accommodate for the cold air, the dry air might be a bit of a problem. This will cause plants to dry out and die, and it's hard for a plant to adapt to these conditions. Ideally, you should have a humidifier nearby, and make sure that it has enough water to take care of the plants.

For cleaning up, you should take every pot or bed that you have and dig up the dead plant. Some plants don't make it, but don't be sad. It just takes a bit of time. You have to get rid of all the dead leaves and roots though, and ideally place it in a forest nearby so that it sinks into the ground. Having it near can harm your plants and it's not ideal, so do away with it as needed.

For watering, you probably won't need to do it all that often, but check your plants. Usually once a week during the harsher months is fine, but do check every single day so you're not wasting time and killing off plants. You should give it a bit of water, but not too much, and fi the soil is wet, avoid watering it. You can then check it each day, and if needed water it again.

And finally, there is weeding. Actually, there isn't weeding. The best part about indoor plants is you almost never have to weed. Occasionally, you might get one that grows there, but you normally don't have this issue except maybe during the spring and summer months. But, during the fall and winter, it's hard for them to thrive, so they will more than likely die off. You should watch out though and handle accordingly.

Conclusion

Thank you again for downloading this book!

I hope I was able to show you a few cool tidbits about how to grow fruit indoors. It's pretty easy, but it does take a bit of skill and practice, so you should learn accordingly and act accordingly. Growing fruit and other plants indoors might seem a bit hard at first, but trying it and learning is the best thing to do. It does take a bit of time, but this book is a great way to get started in this fun hobby. Plus, once you do it well the first time you'll know what to do next, and this hobby will get even more fun and even better than before in no time. Grow what you want, and you can do it inside as well, just follow the steps laid out here and you'll be fine.

Your next step is to actually try doing this yourself. Get everything that you need, and start growing your own fruit indoors. It's a ton of fun, and you'll learn a lot. It might take a little bit, but with ample practice, you will soon learn how to have a green thumb and grow some of your favorite plants.

Container Gardening—

Discover The Baby Steps To Growing Fruit, Vegetables, And Plants In Containers Easily!

Disclaimer
- Although the author and publisher have made every effort to ensure that the information in this book was correct at press time, the author and publisher do not assume and hereby disclaim any liability to any party for any loss, damage, or disruption caused by errors or omissions, whether such errors or omissions result from negligence, accident, or any other cause.
- This book is not intended as a substitute for the medical advice of physicians. The reader should regularly consult a physician in matters relating to his/her health and particularly with respect to any symptoms that may require diagnosis or medical attention.

Copyright 2014 by LOVE AND LIVE LIFE TO THE EXTREME FULLEST PUBLISHING- All rights reserved.

This document is geared towards providing exact and reliable information in regards to the topic and issue covered. The publication is sold with the idea that the publisher is not required to render accounting, officially permitted, or otherwise, qualified services. If advice is necessary, legal or professional, a practiced individual in the profession should be ordered.

- From a Declaration of Principles which was accepted and approved equally by a Committee of the American Bar Association and a Committee of Publishers and Associations.

In no way is it legal to reproduce, duplicate, or transmit any part of this document in either electronic means or in printed format. Recording of this publication is strictly prohibited and any storage of this document is not allowed unless with written permission from the publisher. All rights reserved.

The information provided herein is stated to be truthful and consistent, in that any liability, in terms of inattention or otherwise, by any usage or abuse of any policies, processes, or directions contained within is the solitary and utter responsibility of the recipient reader. Under no circumstances will any legal responsibility or blame be held against the publisher for any reparation, damages, or monetary loss due to the information herein, either directly or indirectly.

Respective authors own all copyrights not held by the publisher.

The information herein is offered for informational purposes solely, and is universal as so. The presentation of the information is without contract or any type of guarantee assurance.

The trademarks that are used are without any consent, and the publication of the trademark is without permission or backing by the trademark owner. All trademarks and brands within this book are for clarifying purposes only and are the owned by the owners themselves, not affiliated with this document.

Have Any Issues With This Book? Contact Randy at Randycfo@triggerhealthyhabits.com For Any Concerns About Quality, Copyright, Trademark, Or any issues or concerns you may have.

Your FREE Gift
Click Here

As a way of saying thank you,

Get your free natural therapeutic remedies report by clicking below.

What you'll receive

Enjoy the rest of the book!

Click here to get your Natural Therapeutic Remedies Report

The Benefits Of Short Reads,

Our Main Mission Is To Provide You With Quality Content In A Short Period Of Time, We Strive To Make Our Books Short And To The Point. These Days Who Has The Time To Read A Big Long Book? We Do Not Write Fiction Books, We Want To Help As Many People As Possible By Providing Them These Handbooks To Help Better Their Lives. We Hope You Enjoy This Kindle Short Reads E-Book

Table Of Contents

CHAPTER 1

CHAPTER 2

CHAPTER 3

CHAPTER 4

CHAPTER 5

CHAPTER 6

CHAPTER 7

CHAPTER 1

Container gardening is a great way to garden in a small space, and there are so many options with container gardening! If versatility is something you desire, then container gardening just might be for you. You can grow plants in about any container at all; so cost is completely dependent on you. My mother has been known to plant flowers in old teapots and soda bottles alike.

Gardening can fall flat for someone with a busy life, though. There is nothing worse than coming home after traveling to find all your plants have been destroyed by pests or withered away from a lack of watering.

Pick planters that are low-cost or even recycle some containers if you want to save costs. If you are planning a flower garden or a garden to improve the appearance of your space, plan on spending a significant amount of your budget on the planting containers. The cost of nice containers can add up quickly! Also, attractive flowering plants are not cheap.

As for planting from seeds, seedling or well-established plant, again, your budget might play a big role in this decision. Seeds are much cheaper. But, if you live in a colder region, growing from seeds may mean beginning your growing season indoors. This could add costs bringing the price of growing from seeds to an amount comparable to growing from seedlings or well-established plants. Buying well-established plants also takes a lot of the guess work out of it.

CHAPTER 2

The climate of your region will greatly affect when you plant outside. In cooler climates, you might have to wait until most of spring is over to know that outside plants will be safe from frost. When purchasing plants or seeds, whether it be online or a supermarket or a nursery, pay close attention to labels. On most labels, it will give instructions specific to your region. The label should be helpful in determining the best time to plant outdoors.

CHAPTER 3

If you picked this book based on its title, I'm going to assume you are new to gardening. I want to help you get your plants going without feeling overwhelmed by information. Once you feel confident with the basics, by all means, keep reading! Let's go over the basic steps to get your plants started in a container.

Now the fun begins! Start filling that container with dirt! Check the plant label again to see how deep the plant's roots are anticipated to grow. This will determine how much potting soil you will need to put in the container. Remember, the soil will settle quite a bit so add a little extra. Once the container is filled enough to meet depth requirements, dig a hole for the plant.

When planting an established plant or seedling, never grab the plant by its stem to transplant it from one container to another.

If you would like to know more about maintaining your container garden, then just keep reading. There are many things to consider with a garden of any kind, and more things to consider depending on what type of garden you have just planted. Do you have all annuals or are some of your plants biennial or perennial? The needs of each plant throughout the growing season and extending into the cold season will vary. Make sure you know what each plant will need. There are some basics to maintaining your brand new garden.

CHAPTER 4

The success or failure of a garden is all in the soil. If the soil being used is lacking nutrients, the plants will not thrive. Nutrient-dense soil that is watered appropriately will grow healthy, robust plants. An important part of creating nutrient-dense soil is fertilizing appropriately. We have developed chemical methods to fertilize our soil; but I suggest taking a look at nature for a lesson in fertilization for a more long-term approach. In the middle of a forest, there isn't a fertilizer fairy going about spraying the soil. Instead, there is a cycle of growth and decay that support each other.

CHAPTER 5

Composting is definitely something you will want to do outside. As you add items like leaves, grass clippings, manure, apple cores and banana peels, you will discover that your compost has an odor that is far from pleasant. Beyond that, compost piles need some sunlight and moisture to break down appropriately. Composting is definitely a long-term commitment, and it shouldn't be started with the thought that you will achieve usable compost quickly. It takes a while for things like leaves and grass and food waste to decompose. It is something that can be started this growing season with the thought that it will help prepare the soil for the next growing season. If you put it on your plants too soon, it can actually destroy the plants.

As for turning that pile of compost, every few weeks ought to do it. The goal behind turning the compost is to ensure that all the compost materials degrade at a similar rate. Typically the top layer and the center layer will not show the same degree of decomposition. Turning also allows air in and keeps materials from clumping.

CHAPTER 6

Keep in mind that plants like cucumbers, zucchini and tomatoes are just a few varieties of vegetables that will need some plant support system. Tomato plants tend to get very tall, and the stems are unable to support the weight of the growing tomatoes as multiple tomatoes appear. There are specific products for tomatoes that resemble cages that can be used to help the plant support the weight of the developing tomatoes. Cucumbers and zucchini

I am especially concerned with using insecticides on my fruits and vegetables. Not only am I concerned about possible human side effects of the handling or ingestion of these chemicals, I am just as concerned about the role it will play on the bug population.

CHAPTER 7

As you continue to watch your garden grow and enjoy the fruits of your labor, you may want to know more about gardening. Here are a few more advanced tips for you to think about.

If you are planting multiple plants in one container, make sure that they are compatible. The container needs to be big enough to allow the root system of each plant to grow properly, and the plants need to have the same sunlight needs unless one plant will shadow the other providing partial sun. Also, some plants cannot be potted with other plants.

Printed in Great Britain
by Amazon.co.uk, Ltd.,
Marston Gate.